# Jack Vance

## Seven Articles on
## His Work and Travels

MICHAEL ANDRE-DRIUSSI

ISBN: 1947614029
ISBN-13: 978-1947614-02-4 (Sirius Fiction)

**\*\*\*\***

"Asi Achih: The Future History of Jack Vance" originally appeared in *The New York Review of Science Fiction No. 113,* January 1998.

"*The Blue World:* Jack Vance's Hard Science Wonder" originally appeared in *The New York Review of Science Fiction No. 125,* January 1999.

"The Adventures of Jack Vance Traveling and Writing" originally appeared in *The New York Review of Science Fiction No. 302,* October 2013.

"Tracing terms in Jack Vance's 'Sjambak'" originally appeared in *The New York Review of Science Fiction No. 311,* July 2014.

"Patterns to the Five Demon Princes of Jack Vance" originally appeared in *The New York Review of Science Fiction No. 325,* September 2015.

"'The New Prime' as Herald of Future Jack Vance" originally appeared in *The New York Review of Science Fiction No. 326,* October 2015.

"Review of *An Encyclopedia of Jack Vance*" originally appeared in *Journal of the Fantastic in the Arts No. 15.3,* 2004.

# CONTENTS

# *ASI ACHIH:* THE FUTURE HISTORY OF JACK VANCE

The term "future history" brings to mind the works of Asimov and Stapledon among others, but not the fiction of Jack Vance. After all, Vance is not using a quasi-scientific discipline like "psychohistory," cycles of history, or speculative future evolution as an overarching structure to tell a story (ultimately about the discipline itself). In fact, the idea of Vance's sf as a future history is met with laughter, dismissed out of hand — there are no galactic empires in "Vance Space," and hence they do not rise, stagnate, nor fall; as such there is simply no galactic history. In novel after novel, Vance drives home the impression that all history is local in scale, provincial in focus, and basically the same sorry mess as the post-colonial world.

Granted, then, it is a crazy idea that seems to go directly against the spirit of the fiction. Where whimsy meets a challenge: another mad quest. Thus and why-for the title of this essay, "asi achih," the term of fatalistic resignation uttered by the men of Dar Sai upon returning home each day from the mines: "And so it went."[1]

(I will cover thirty novels and one novelette, but none of the short stories. Also excluded are *The Many Worlds of Magnus Ridolph,*[2] *Monsters in Orbit, The Houses of Iszm, Slaves of the Klau,* and *The Brains of Earth.*)

Let us begin with the works in which dates are explicitly mentioned. Vance Space appears to have two highly defined epochs: the Oikumene period of the Demon Princes series (five novels) and the much later Gaean Reach period of the Alastor Cluster (three novels), the Cadwal Chronicles (three novels), and four other novels.

The Demon Princes novels give all sorts of historical tidbits in the various articles and footnotes. In prehistoric times the alien Star Kings visited Earth, gathered up a group of Neanderthals and took them back to planet Ghnarumen, where they used them as evolutionary goads via blood sport. Tens of thousands of years of this competition changed both species; the Star Kings finally gained the upper hand and returned to Earth their humans, a group we refer to as "Cro-Magnon." So the Star Kings are revealed to have had a hand in the evolution *of Homo sapiens sapiens.*

A note in chapter seven of *Star King* (the first Demon Princes novel) tells us that the space age begins with Year Zero at A.D. 2000 (Old Style). The space age has been going on for a thousand years prior to the invention of the Jarnell

---

1. "The essayist attempts to assert authority over the reader by using an obscure foreign phrase in the title, and then, rather than explaining said phrase immediately, rolls out a number of fantastic names and concepts to further mystify those who have not yet stopped reading from boredom. A quaint archaic 'why-for,' to set the teeth on edge, before finally, the answer long awaited, a phrase nonsensical in this context. This amounts to a clumsy effort by a person fearful of being exposed as the charlatan he really is." —Sistie Fael, *The Outlook*

2. "An unfortunate decision of omission, since Magnus Ridolph is the quintessential Vancean hero, a natural lord among men."—McFarquhar Kenshaw, *The Gaean*

Intersplit star drive in 1020, and there is a note stating that ninety or more extra-solar planets have been colonized (ch. 3), including those of such distant stars as Rigel, 1,000 light years away (Krokinole, Rigel XIV, referenced as being inhabited in year 1000 [ch. 1]), by way of some pre-Jarnell star drive(s). The action in *Star King* takes place in 1524 of the space age (ch. 10), and the four other Demon Princes novels follow at one-year intervals. In the course of the five novels, passing reference is made twice (ch. 7; *Killing Machine,* ch. 11) to the planet Sirene, the setting for the novelette "The Moon Moth," bringing this memorable world into the compass of the Oikumene.[3]

Three known groups hold the Oikumene together: the Institute (an academy bent on hoarding and restricting the flow of information), the Jarnell Corporation (sole manufacturers of the Intersplit, the most advanced ftl star drive of the time), and the IPCC (Interplanetary Police Cooperation Company, a sort of Interpol in space). Notable figures of the Oikumene include Baron Bodissey, author of the multivolume *Life,* and the mad poet Navarth (who actually appears as a character in *The Palace of Love,* the third Demon Princes volume). The Oikumene has no rival star cultures, alien or human. The Star Kings of Ghnarumen are independent yet incorporated into the Oikumene — the Beyond is a wide-open frontier converted into pirate kingdoms by the Demon Princes in 1500. The interstellar currency is the SVU (Standard Value Unit).

In what year of the space age does the Oikumene come into existence? A tricky question: does the Oikumene predate its own triad? The IPCC is established in 1075 (also the date of the earliest extant use of the term "Oikumene"); the Jarnell Intersplit is discovered in 1020; and the Institute

---

3. "Details matter—precision is everything! While 'The Moon Moth' does have something called simply the Institute, still and unfortunately the interstellar government is not 'the Oikumene' but 'the Home Planets.'"—Lionel Wistofer, *The Monstrator*

traces its own origins to the year Zero. To avoid hairsplitting I've placed the beginning of the Oikumene at 500, the earliest alluded-to date of colonization (the lost world of Thamber [*Killing Machine,* ch. 9] in the Demon Princes series).

When does the Oikumene end, and under what circumstances? It may end relatively soon after the close of the Demon Princes series: Albert B. Hall, in a preface to *A Concise History of the Oikumene* (publication date unknown), writes:

> For more than a thousand years … the human race has swept across space…. But now there is stasis in the Oikumene, with many comings and goings, and it seems that perhaps the pendulum is about to swing back.
>
> The Oikumene may be forced to expand. Other Oikumenes may come into existence. Conceivably men may collide with the realm of another race, for there is abundant evidence that other space-traveling peoples have gone before us, how and why to disappear no one can say (*Killing Machine,* ch. 7).

From a period of stasis, a period of change is anticipated. There are several hints of different forms of change on the Oikumene's horizon: the Institute is being publicly challenged by the Planned Progress League in a televised debate in 1521 (if the League succeeds, the resulting information explosion could prove destabilizing to the Oikumene); Kirth Gersen's massive counterfeiting in 1526 may have destabilized the SVU in fact or by example; the Institute has been further weakened by the upper echelon assassination by which a Demon Prince nearly gained control of the Institute in 1528; and the elimination of the Demon Princes means that the Beyond is no longer a nest of pirate kingdoms containing the Oikumene and preying upon it (explosive growth in trade and exploration seems probable).

For whatever reasons, it seems that the Oikumene did end at some point. The most probable details will develop as we continue.

The other galactic-history Rosetta Stone for Vance Space is the prologue to *The Gray Prince.* Here the term "Gaean Reach" appears for the first time; the Reach and Alastor Cluster are shown to be contemporary cultures. In addition we discover that "the space age is thirty thousand years old" (*Gray Prince,* prologue). We may deduce that the other Gaean Reach novels — *Maske: Thaery, Galactic Effectuator,* the Cadwal Chronicles (*Araminta Station, Ecce and Old Earth, Throy*), and *Night Lamp* — and the Alastor Cluster novels (*Trullion, Marune, Wyst*) share a single historical setting.

Therefore the Gaean Reach would appear to be the successor to the Oikumene. Of the triad holding human interstellar civilization together, one element is now missing, one has been superseded, and one remains unchanged. Missing is the Institute, as there does not seem to be any evidence of an Institute on Old Earth, or anywhere else in the Gaean Reach. Superseded is the Jarnell Corporation, it would seem, since there is no mention of the Jarnell Intersplit star drive: Gaean starships go into "whisk" (*Trullion,* ch. 2) using "Intertwist" engines (*Maske: Thaery,* ch. 11). Unchanged is the IPCC, the only triad group to survive: the IPCC plays a part in the Cadwal Chronicles, *Maske: Thaery, Galactic Effectuator,* and *Night Lamp.* The cultural legacy of the Oikumene has apparently fared better, since both Baron Bodissey and the mad poet Navarth are frequently alluded to in novels of the Gaean Reach.

(In fact, Baron Bodissey's *Life* is an interesting case: six volumes [*Killing Machine,* ch. 10] when first assailed by pundits; grown to seven [*The Face,* ch. 8] in 1527, then eight volumes [*Book of Dreams,* ch. 18] by 1528; periodically appearing in the Gaean Reach as "a truncated version of Baron Bodissey's ten volume *Life"* [*Ecce and Old Earth,* ch.

7.1]. Furthermore, knowledgeable people of the Gaean Reach often quote Baron Bodissey to each other in times of trouble or absurdity — he has grown in stature to become the Homer or Confucius of a later civilization.)

Where the Oikumene stood alone in the galaxy, the Gaean Reach has company: Alastor Cluster, the Erdic Realms (*Wyst,* ch. 3), and the Primarchic (*Wyst,* ch. 10) are all (presumably) human star cultures, but the Olefract Empire and the Liss Empire are alien and hostile to the Gaean Reach (*Galactic Effectuator,* ch. 2).[4] *Galactic Effectuator* has a definite "cold war" feel — the planet Maz, borderland between three starfaring cultures, is divided into sectors like those of postwar Berlin. Tensions are high, and "incidents" can have far-reaching consequences, perhaps even the apocalyptic warfare of a "World War Three" among the stars. For these reasons I situate *Galactic Effectuator* at the end of the Gaean Reach sequence.

The currencies of the Gaean Reach are the SVU, another survivor of Oikumene times (in *Maske: Thaery,* ch. 11; *Wyst,* ch. 3); the SLU or "Standard Labor Unit" (in *Galactic Effectuator,* ch. 2; *The Gray Prince,* ch. 2); and the Sol (in the Cadwal Chronicles and *Night Lamp).* (The currency of Alastor Cluster is the ozol.)

Having placed the fifteen novels and one novelette that have clear historical markers, we now move into the murkier region of novels that do not give explicit dates. In these cases we will watch for one or more of the following details:

1) the duration of "human history" at the time of the novel;
2) referencing to another Vance novel;
3) the duration of a given planet's colonization;
4) knowledge of Old Earth as origin of humankind;

---

4. "*Galactic Effectuator* offers a watered-down version of the Magnus Ridolph masterpiece 'The Kokod Warriors.' Scholars of true merit must rescue Magnus Ridolph from obscurity before it is too late!"—McFarquhar Kenshaw

5) monetary units.

Whether or not any one of these novels is in the same universe as the Oikumene/Gaean Reach is debatable.

With regard to the starting point of human history, I don't know what date Vance is thinking of, but barring earthshaking new discoveries real or fictional we can say that History begins at Sumer, 3500 B.C. Which translates into the year -5500 of the space age.

Now then, let's survey the novels.

The *Planet of Adventure* or "Tschai" series provides a mother lode of prehistorical details (remembering to convert from Tschai years to Earth years by multiplying Tschai years by 1.336). The anchor point is given when our hero states "Human history on Earth goes back ten thousand years" (*City of the Chasch,* ch. 2), which plants the series at year 4500.[5] In Tschai history myriad ancient alien star empires rose and fell; early humans were brought to Tschai as slaves and tens of thousands of years later their descendants have no idea of a human homeworld. The monetary unit on Tschai is the plant-grown "sequin."

*Space Opera* may be in the Oikumene/Gaean Reach universe. Earth history is six thousand years old (ch. 10), fixing the novel at year 500. *Space Opera* hinges upon a prehistoric starfaring culture of proto-Welsh who build a starship and colonize a planet of a distant star before slipping into obscurity — a Vancean version of the Atlantis motif. The novel starts and ends on Earth, where the currency is the dollar (well, cents at least [ch. 2]).

*The Five Gold Bands* probably isn't in the Oikumene/Gaean Reach universe, since the background scenario is too different: the Langtry star drive, the only star drive available, is a monopoly controlled by the five sons of

---

5. "If the Tschai novels take place against the backdrop of the Oikumene, where the cosmopolitan worlds of Rigel are 1,000 light years from Earth, then why would hero Adam Reith think, 'Men and women, on a world two hundred and twelve light-years from Earth!' (*City of the Chasch,* ch. 2)"—Lionel Wistofer

Langtry, each of whom started a new human-made-alien species. But it may fit into the pre-Jarnell Intersplit period of the Oikumene. Earth is known and is being held down; the interstellar currency is the mark.

*Big Planet* has been an Earth colony for five hundred years, pegging the novel at year 500 at the earliest. Local money is iron.

*Emphyrio* features the planet Halma, a human colony for 3,500 years, suggesting it is set in year 3500 at the earliest (I place it at year 4500 for reasons given later). But it may properly belong to the post-Gaean period, since local history mentions "star wars," a feature of what I am considering as post-Gaean novels. In addition there is the post-Gaean detail of uncertainty as to the origin world of humankind: "Some declared Earth to be the source of human migration; another group inclined toward Triptolemus; others pointed to Amenaro" (ch. 19). Likewise the offworld currencies "sequin" (ch. 15) and "valuta" (ch. 16) match neither the SVU of the Oikumene nor any of the Gaean Reach/Alastor Cluster currencies.

On the other hand, *Emphyrio* pivots upon the Historical Institute of Earth (ch. 19), which forges a direct link to the Historical Institute of Earth in the Durdane trilogy (*The Anome, The Brave Free Men, The Asutra*), which might also be related to Breakness Institute of *The Languages of Pao,* and/or most importantly, a connection to the Institute that plays such a large background role in the Oikumene of the Demon Princes series.

Another link between different Vance novels is found in the play "Emphyrio," enacted by puppets in *Emphyrio* (ch. 2) and mentioned in passing in *Showboat World* (ch. 1). So the cluster of "Emphyrio"/Historical Institute novels is made up of *Emphyrio,* the Durdane trilogy, *Showboat World,* and *Big Planet* (since *Showboat World* is the second novel set upon the world Big Planet), with suggestive ties to the Institutes of Pao and Oikumene.

*Showboat World* begins with an excerpt from a reference

book (*Handbook of the Inhabited Worlds*), similar to the Oikumene style of the Demon Princes series, yet the title of the work is not familiar, nor is its planet of publication given. *Showboat World* has no clear historical markers (beyond the play "Emphyrio") yet is generally assumed to be taking place thousands of years after *Big Planet*.

Planet Pao of *The Languages of Pao* has been colonized for five thousand years (ch. 18), calibrating it at circa year 5000. Pao is also located in the Polymark Cluster, and the "Polymarks" are stars mentioned in passing in the Gaean Reach's *Night Lamp* (p. 201).

Planet Durdane of the Durdane trilogy is dated at 9000+ S.A. since it has been colonized from Earth for nine thousand years (*The Anome,* ch. 9).[6] (Durdane's money is the florin.)

The Blue World has been colonized for only about two hundred years, but because the colonists were prisoners being transported to a different planet, and such transportation historically is a form of colonization that comes later rather than sooner, the novel *The Blue World* doesn't fit within the Oikumene. There are no real historical markers among these science-fictional Botany Bay/Pitcairn Islanders. There is no currency on the Blue World, though food sponges may come close in bartering usage.

Together this group (*Big Planet, Planet of Adventure, Showboat World, Emphyrio,* the Durdane trilogy, and *The Blue*

---

6. "Once again the textual evidence is there for those who deign to read the source material: in *The Asutra* the human star culture is neither the Oikumene nor the Gaean Reach, it is 'the Pan-Humanic League' (ch. 3). Also, the Asutra themselves are the first technologically competent nonhuman creatures the Historical Institute has encountered (ch. 3); shall we forget the highly competent alien Star Kings of the Oikumene? Lastly and most damaging, Earth is legendary on Durdane (*The Anome,* ch. 9), a trait that this befuddled pseudo-scholar uses to tag 'Post Gaean Era' novels! If we cannot have accuracy, can we at least have consistency?"—Lionel Wistofer

*World)* makes up a transitional period between Oikumene and Gaean Reach, or so I propose, and I call this era "the Middle Millennia."[7] To avoid overlap with the Oikumene I start the Middle Millennia at 2500 with the writing of the Emphyrio legend, though it could have been written as early as the Demon Princes era, circa 1500.

In some respects the Historical Institute stands to Vance Space as the Church stood to medieval Europe: a scholarly preserver and distributor of knowledge; an intelligence network; a protean political empire that failed to fill the vacuum left by the collapse of the Roman Empire. The Historical Institute of *Emphyrio,* Durdane, and *The Languages of Pao* is not nearly as secretive with its data-hoard as the Institute — one only has to ask and the scholars will tell all sorts of things. The Historical Institute of *Emphyrio* and Durdane also has an official "non-interference" policy similar to Star Trek's "Prime Directive," but logically this then necessitates the use of local spies (in *Emphyrio)* and offworlders disguised as locals (in Durdane). Breakness Institute of *The Languages of Pao* exhibits no such policy; to the contrary, Lord Palafox of Breakness Institute seems expansionistic in his designs for Pao, yet it is his secret harem that seems to be the unforgivable sin in the eyes of his institute. Not content with disseminating world-warping knowledge, he wants to inseminate the population until there will be "only Palafox and the seed of Palafox on Pao" (ch. 19). He is thwarted in his ambitions.

---

7. "One might just as easily make the following links: *Planet of Adventure* series and *Emphyrio;* Durdane trilogy and *To Live Forever; Space Opera* and *Emphyrio.* Why? Because the first set has sequins as a monetary unit; the second has florins as currency; and the third features an Earth where ancient Athens is restored. It then follows that since sets one and three both contain *Emphyrio,* voilà, textual evidence proving that *Planet of Adventure, Emphyrio,* and *Space Opera* share the same universe! All very creative, but scholars should avoid creativity at all costs."—Sistie Fael

An additional parallel between Europe's middle ages and the Middle Millennia is found in the figure of Emphyrio, an authentic savior who is, surprisingly (for those accustomed to Vance's usual religious satire), less like King Arthur than he is like Jesus Christ. The legendary Emphyrio is an "authentic" savior because the text establishes that he really existed (no sham there), he really performed a technologically-aided miracle in converting alien bio-engineered warriors (Wirwan) into peaceful hermits (no sham), he was killed for preaching peace (no sham), yet his message outlived him and won that phase of the struggle (no sham). (This is almost shockingly different from every other religion depicted in Vance Space, since every one of them is exposed as a show to cow and milk the masses. Then again, perhaps the semi-Gnostic Emphyrio escapes the satiric scythe by the fact that he has no organized religion following him?)[8] It would appear that Emphyrio stands to the Middle Millennia as Jesus stood to medieval Europe, albeit in a vastly diminished form.

Finally, we come to the end of Vance's sfnal history, a time I term "the Post-Gaean Period." This phase is characterized by a mingling of science fiction and fantasy, a stage beyond which begins the fantasy-drenched aeons of *The Dying Earth.*

*To Live Forever* is a novel about using clones and personality transfer to achieve immortality, two technologies which appear nowhere else in the fictions being discussed. The Earth of *To Live Forever* seems changed

---

8. "Another bit of fatuous waggery, on par with the trite phrase 'All Vance novels are revenge novels,' by which one jackanapes recognizes another. Stuff and poppycock! Jack Vance is quite obviously an evangelical Druid. Does he ridicule organized religions? Yes, all of them (especially those found in India), with the exception of Druidism! Does he show that religious miracles are all fakery to beguile the believers? Yes, but not the one religion that produces real results—Druidism! See 'Son of the Tree,' *Maske: Thaery,* 'Noise,' among several others."—Sistie Fael

nearly beyond recognition, in contrast to the familiar world of Oikumene and Gaean Reach times, and yet starflight seems to be in its infancy — though perhaps this is a rediscovery rather than a first invention. The altered geography (a landscape more alien than that of *The Last Castle)* and unusual technology both argue for the Post-Gaean, the early starflight argues for the Oikumene, pre-Jarnell Intersplit. (The currency is the florin.)

*The Dragon Masters* is set on the distant planet Aerlith. Aerlith has been colonized by the human exiles of the War of Ten Stars, a conflict that saw the Nightmare Coalition defeat the Old Rule, also known as the Human Empire (ch. 4). This star war seems to have happened several hundred years ago — perhaps exactly 812 years ago, if it was in fact the trigger that set the autochthonous sacerdotes on their secret quest to build a starship with which to repopulate the devastated galaxy. Certainty regarding the human homeworld has been lost — candidates are Earth, Eden, and Tempe (ch. 12). The hero hopes to quickly re-attain the ability of starflight, despite his culture's current Renaissance level of technological development.

The technology of bioengineering is a common enough thread through the history of Vance Space — the five new human species of *The Five Gold Bands;* the accidental new species of Fojos on Boniface (*The Book of Dreams,* ch. 8); the numerous created servitors and mistakes on Fader in *Night Lamp;* etc. But in *The Dragon Masters* this technology takes on a highly recognizable element of fantasy as the bio-engineered soldiers have the forms of dragons, signaling the transition in the galaxy from modes of sf to those of fantasy.

The circle is closed with *The Last Castle,* where Earth has been razed by the Six Star War and re-colonized by humans from Altair after 3,000 years. Again, as in *The Dragon Masters,* the trappings of fantasy (talking birds used for aerial transport; power wagons that are syrup-drinking slabs of living muscle harnessed to drive trains; etc.) shift the tenor toward that of *The Dying Earth,* a quasi-medieval fantasy with elements of science fiction. The hero's society has no starflight ability, having given such things over to their servitors, but in the end the humans want to relearn this and other technical skills.

Are the War of Ten Stars and the Six Star Wars related, perhaps different movements of the same conflict? Is the Nightmare Coalition of *The Dragon Masters* made up of an alliance between the Olefract and Liss Empires of *Galactic Effectuator*? It is impossible to say with certainty, but I suspect they are. In any event, I place *The Last Castle* after *The Dragon Masters* in the Post-Gaean Period if only because the former has a greater stretch of local history, nearly 4,000 years.

Looking over this tentative timeline, a patchwork of local histories anchored at points by galactic history, it seems that we have a pre-space age dominated by aliens; a muddled early space age of human expansion among the stars; the emergence of the Oikumene as the first human interstellar civilization on a peerless frontier; an interregnum featuring some interstellar conflicts among aliens; the blossoming of the Gaean Reach and its neighbors; and one or more apocalyptic star wars leading to the final collapse of human science at the threshold of magic. Almost straight Toynbee, but minus all the praise of religion, naturally — this is Jack Vance, after all. Growth, Empire, Interregnum, Rebirth, Collapse: and so it went.

•

## Tentative Unified Timeline for "Vance Space"

### Year: Event
-9.3 meg: Pnume history begins on Tschai.
-? meg: Shivvan invade Tschai.
-? meg: Gjee invade Tschai.
-? meg: Fesa invade Tschai.
-? meg: Hsi invade Tschai.

-129,000: Old Chasch arrive on Tschai (*City of the Chasch,* ch. 4)

-119,000: Blue Chasch arrive on Tschai, fight Old Chasch; Green Chasch introduced as shock troops (*City of the Chasch,* ch. 4).

-99,000: Star Kings visit Earth, take Neanderthals (*Star King,* ch. 8).

-74,500: Dirdir arrive on Tschai, fight Chasch to stalemate (*City of the Chasch,* ch. 4).

-65,500: Dirdir bring first humans (proto-Mongol) to Tschai; escaped humans mutate into Marshmen (*City of the Chasch,* ch. 2).

-49,000: Star Kings drop off "Cro-Magnons" on Earth (*Star King,* ch. 8).

-27,500: Proto-Welsh build ship, go to planet Yan (*Space Opera,* ch. 10).

-22,500: Emergence of Steppe humans on Tschai; Old Chasch enter senescence on Tschai; Dirdir bring proto-Caucasians to Tschai (*City of the Chasch,* ch. 4).

-8500: Wankh arrive on Tschai, fight Dirdir.

-5500: Earth history begins at Sumer (3500 B.C.)

0: Year A.D. 2000 (Old Style). Space Age begins (*Star King,* ch. 7).

?: *The Five Gold Bands* (Langtry: early star drive).

300: Yan dissidents crash in Wales (*Space Opera,* ch. 10).

500: *Space Opera* (6,000 years of human history; interstellar travel at one light year per day).

500+: *Big Planet* (Earth colony 500 years).

## The Oikumene

### Year: Event

500: Planet Thamber colonized (*Killing Machine,* ch. 9).

734: *Cosmopolis* magazine launched (*Palace of Love,* ch. 1).

993: Ninety inhabited planets (*Star King,* ch. 3).

1000: Planet Krokinole (Rigel XIV) referenced (*Star King,* ch. 1).

1020: (circa) Jarnell Intersplit discovered — starflight much faster (*Star King*, ch. 8).

?: "The Moon Moth"

1028: Valhalla (at Tau Gemini) referenced (*Star King*, ch. 3).

1075: Birth of IPCC (Interworld Police Coordination Company) (*Star King*, chap. 3).

1292: *Popular Handbook of the Planets* (edition 303) published (*Star King*, ch. 4).

1479: Smade colonizes Smade's Planet (*Star King*, ch. 1).

1499: The five Demon Princes raid Mount Pleasant (*Star King*, ch. 10).

1500: Conclave of Demon Princes at Smade's Planet, where they divide the Beyond (*Star King*, ch. 10); the Texahoma Riots (*Killing Machine*, ch. 5).

1521: Televised debate between representatives of the Institute and the Planned Progress League (*Palace of Love*, ch. 10, 11).

1523: *Cosmopolis* article on Smade of Smade's Planet (*Star King*, ch. 1); Howard Allan Treesong nearly gains control of IPCC (*Book of Dreams*, ch. 1).

1524: *Star King* (ch. 1).

1525: *Handbook to the Planets* (348th edition) published (*Palace of Love*, ch. 3); *Killing Machine* (ch. 1).

1526: *Palace of Love* (ch. 1).

1527: *The Face* takes place (assumed).

1528: *The Book of Dreams* takes place (assumed); Howard Allan Treesong nearly gains control of the Institute.

1530: The tenth volume of Baron Bodissey's *Life* published; *The Demon Princes* by Caril Carphen (*Star King*, ch. 10) published by Elucidarian Press of Vega (guesses).

## The Middle Millennia

**Year: Event**

2500: Emphyrio legend written (*Emphyrio*, ch. 19).

2500+: *Showboat World* (mentions play "Emphyrio" in ch.

1).

4300: Golden Yao (humans) of Tschai broadcast space message until the Dirdir crush them.

4500: *Planet of Adventure (City of the Chasch, Servants of the Wankh, The Dirdir, The Pnume)* set with 10,000 years of human history (*City of the Chasch,* ch. 2).

4500: *Emphyrio* (colonized for 3,500 years, ch. 20).

5000+: *Languages of Pao* (colonized for 5,000 years, ch. 18).

9000+: Durdane series (*The Anome, The Brave Free Men, The Asutra)* colonized for 9,000 years (*Anome,* ch. 9).

?: *The Blue World*

## The Gaean Reach

**Year: Event**

25,000: Planet Fader colonized (*Night Lamp).*

29,000: Count Sarbert founds the Naturalist Society (*Ecce and Old Earth,* ch. 6); planet Wyst colonized (*Wyst,* ch. 1).

29,800: The Submission Treaties of Koryphon (*Gray Prince* prologue).

30,000: Alastor Cluster novels (*Trullion, Marune, Wyst).* The Cadwal Chronicles (*Araminta Station, Ecce and Old Earth, Throy). The Gray Prince. Maske: Thaery. Night Lamp. Galactic Effectuator* (Gaean Reach's hostile borders).

## Post-Gaean Period

**Year: Event**

?: *To Live Forever*

?: *The Dragon Masters.* 812 Aerlith years ago, sacerdotes begin building their ship. Twelve generations ago, Happy Valley was dominant when the Basics first arrive. Eleven generations ago, the Age of Wet Iron. After five years of peace, the return of the Basics.

?: *The Last Castle.* 3700 years before, the Six Star War leaves

Earth fallow for 3000 years. Seven hundred years before, Lords from Altair build nine Castles on Earth. Five hundred years before, Old Hagedorn demolished and rebuilt.

•

From *Anome* to *Wyst:* the "Vance Space" Works

1953: *The Five Gold Bands*
1956: *To Live Forever*
1957: *Big Planet*
1958: *The Languages of Pao*
1961: "The Moon Moth"
1963: *The Dragon Masters*
1964: *Star King* (Demon Princes I)
1964: *The Killing Machine* (Demon Princes II)
1965: *Space Opera*
1966: *The Blue World*
1967: *The Last Castle*
1967: *The Palace of Love* (Demon Princes III)
1968: *City of the Chasch* (Tschai I)
1969: *Emphyrio*
1969: *Servants of the Wankh* (Tschai II)
1969: *The Dirdir* (Tschai III)
1970: *The Pnume* (Tschai IV)
1973: *The Anome* (Durdane I)
1973: *The Brave Free Men* (Durdane II)
1973: *Trullion: Alastor 2262*
1974: *The Asutra* (Durdane III)
1975: *The Gray Prince*
1975: *Marune: Alastor 933*
1975: *Showboat World* (Big Planet II)
1976: *Maske: Thaery*
1978: *Wyst: Alastor 1716*
1979: *The Face* (Demon Princes IV)
1980: *Galactic Effectuator*

1981: *The Book of Dreams* (Demon Princes V)
1987: *Araminta Station* (Cadwal I)
1991: *Ecce and Old Earth* (Cadwal II)
1992: *Throy* (Cadwal III)
1996: *Night Lamp*

# *THE BLUE WORLD:* JACK VANCE'S HARD SCIENCE WONDER

Jack Vance won the Science Fiction and Fantasy Writers of America's Grand Master Award last year [1998], and in belated celebration of this, I'd like to remind everyone of one of his neglected works, the science-fiction novel *The Blue World* (1966).

*The Blue World* is an unusual Vance planetary romance. Yes, it has the exotic location, the low technology level, and the quaintly curious local society that has evolved with these conditions as well as whatever quirks were brought from the homeworld — in short, all the things we have come to expect from Vancean sf.

But the novel is an example of extremes: an extremely exotic location, an extremely low technology level, and an extremely curious society. Further, it is *the* Vance hard sf novel, using both established science and carefully extrapolated science as its backbone, in addition to charting the scientific spirit of inquiry and experimentation.

The main character, Sklar Hast, is a heroic iconoclast, not a rogue like Apollon Zamp of *Showboat World* or Cugel the Clever of *The Eyes of the Overworld;* nor an antihero like

Kirth Gerson of the Demon Princes series; nor is he taught by hard knocks to deny the heroic impulse like Adam Reith of the Planet of Adventure series. Sklar's climactic triumph against the god monster King Kragen is accomplished through that hoariest of sf clichés, an elaborate death machine — and Vance does not usually devote so much energy to describing "hard science" style artifacts.

In fact, it is easy to glibly categorize Vance's novels as being "anti-heroic," "picaresque," "soft science," and "always about revenge." *The Blue World*, however, has a strong narrative, has heroic hard science slaying false gods, and instead of straightforward revenge it has clearly displaced aggression. (Sklar's putative nemesis, the god monster, eats some of Sklar's food, but that is hardly enough to warrant Sklar's reaction. Instead, Sklar's true rival is a priest of the god monster, and with the death of the monster, the priest's rank diminishes, and thereby he loses his suitability to marry a woman Sklar loves.)

The way that Vance accomplishes this in perfect Vancean form is, of course, a tour de force. *The Blue World* takes place on a nameless planet entirely covered with water. The human colonists live on "floats," surface-floating pads of aquatic plants in the equatorial ocean "shallows" that are 300 feet deep (53). A glimpse of Jack Fantasist: positing a world of lily-pad living *à la Thumbelina;* and to complete that image, here comes the local monster form to take the place of the bullfrog — the kragen. "King Kragen bulked on the float like a toad on a lily pad" (49). With four vanes, the kragen swims like a man doing the breaststroke. It is equipped with a gaping maw fed by quick tentacles, and in place of a head it has a bony carapace.

### Hard SF: Welcome to the Bone Age
The lack of dry land means that the tropical island paradise has a big disadvantage to overcome. No land means "no clay to make pottery, no silica for glass, no limestone for concrete, no ore from which to smelt metal" (122). So the

first task is to show how these people live a stone-age lifestyle without a single stone. This seems a task for hard sf.

Allen Steele in *The Encyclopedia of Science Fiction* defines hard sf this way:

> Hard sf is the form of imaginative literature that uses either established or carefully extrapolated science as its backbone … perhaps the most important thing about it is, not that it should include real science in any great detail, but that it should respect the scientific spirit; it should seek to provide natural rather than supernatural or transcendental explanations for the events and phenomena it describes.

Now then, back to the Blue World — how do they live without stone, metal, and clay? The answer is they use a lot of plant materials: "withe," which is like bamboo; pad-skin, which can provide a tough skin for boats or buildings, or when scraped and stretched can become transparent for windows; plant fiber rope, used in the construction of towers, huts, and boats, as well as fishing nets. There are resins for varnish and for cloudy magnifying lenses that allow crude telescopes. One of the more startling-yet-logical materials in use on the floats is human bone — corpses are put into a special harbor where the flesh is stripped by animals. It is tempting to call their technological level of development a "bone age," but "bone" and "stone" age both bring to mind preliterate societies. The floats are not only literate, poring over the written histories of the Firsts (first generation colonists), they also have an ingenious network of semaphore towers linking all the floats with nearly instantaneous communication.

Vance deftly shows how these things are accomplished and avoids turning the society into a showcase from either *The Flintstones* or *Gilligan's Island*.

Aside from the lack of surface land, another problem facing the humans is the giant native life form called kragen — sea monsters. To deal with these despoilers of food-sponge arbors, a priestly caste known as the Intercessors arose. They offer food sacrifice to one big sea monster, King Kragen, in the hope that it will chase off or kill all smaller kragen, which it does. And so it has been for a dozen generations.

Enter the iconoclast: our hero, Sklar Hast. He is an accomplished semaphorist of a good family and thus a princeling of the float he lives on. One day Sklar tries to kill a small kragen he finds eating his sponges. This marks Sklar as a dangerous heretic, since he is trespassing on behavior reserved for King Kragen. King Kragen shows up, easily kills the little kragen, and proceeds to eat Sklar's sponges. Sklar becomes determined to kill King Kragen, but he and his fellows only wound King Kragen with their first attempt — a collapsing-tower deadfall trap.

This attempt at deicide makes the Intercessors demand the death penalty for the conspirators, but the conspirators opt for exile instead, sailing away from the Home Floats to locate and colonize some wild floats. But they remain steadfast in their desire to kill King Kragen — shades of *Moby-Dick*.

Here is where the Hard Science blooms: how to kill King Kragen? Through research of ancestral texts, experimentation, and observation, they come to believe that they need metal (which they know of through a few priceless heirlooms) and electricity (of which they have no experience). To generate electricity they must first have metal and acid; to store acid they must have glass; to make acid they must have electricity. A paradoxical circle — a Bootstrap Scenario.

They build a solar smelter using a water lens (a non-rigid "window" padskin is held horizontal and water is poured into its center; it flexes into a bowl and thereby assumes a lens shape that can focus the sun's rays into a point of concentrated energy). They burn materials in this smelter to find what sort of new substances they might obtain: husks of sea-ooze or local plankton produce a crude glass (that can be formed into flasks); human blood gives iron; kragen blood gives copper.

To make the acid for the batteries they develop a "Rous machine" that uses "cataphoresis" to produce a small amount of electricity from water, said electricity being enough to magnetize compass needles (another new invention) and disassociate seawater to produce the acid of salt.

## The Rous Machine
This Rous machine is the key to the whole enterprise — is it a plausible device or a "ruse"? In the text, the hero meets with his chief engineer and examines the dingus:

> Sklar Hast inspected the clumsy apparatus. A tube of hollow stalk five inches in diameter, supported by a scaffold, rose twenty feet into the air. The base was held at one end of a long box containing what appeared to be wet ashes. The far end of the box was closed by a slab of compressed carbon, into which were threaded copper wires. At the opposite end, between the tube and the wet ashes, was another slab of compressed carbon.
>
> "This is admittedly a crude device … it produces electricity without metal, through the agency of water pressure. Brunet describes … the process [as] 'cataphoresis.' The tube is filled with water, which is thereby forced through the mud, which here is a mixture of ashes and sea-slime. The water carries an electric charge which it communicates to the porous carbon as it seeps through. By this means a small but steady and quite dependable source of electricity is at hand." (170)

Since I'm not an engineer, I looked up "cataphoresis" in the OED. The second meaning is synonymous with "electrophoresis," with an example from 1944 *Electronic Engineering:* "When a solid particle becomes suspended in a liquid medium of higher dielectric constant it becomes, in general, negatively charged relative to the dispersion medium and will therefore be attracted to the anode of an electrode system placed in the solution. This phenomenon is known as cataphoresis."

Naturally I also looked up "electrophoresis," which is the migration of colloidal particles suspended in a liquid under the influence of an electric field, with an example from 1957 *Science News:* "When a charged particle of colloidal dimensions is suspended in a liquid between two charged electrodes, it moves towards the electrode with a charge opposite its own.... This is known as electrophoresis."

Thus cataphoresis is the movement of particles in a fluid toward an electrode — how electricity carries along the particles. The Rous machine as described seems to be something different: the water is forced through mud (possibly a colloid solution), where it picks up an electric charge and carries it to the porous carbon end blocks — the water seeps through and the electrical charge is captured by the copper wires.

Searching for more, I went to the Engineering Library at the University of California, Berkeley. Granted, I should have gone to the Chemistry Library. In any event, I could find no leads on a Rous machine (Rous is connected to medical science but not electrical engineering), and "cataphoresis" is now used for medical science.

So I cannot tell if the Rous machine would really work or not. But by the following reasoning, perhaps it can work: an electrical motor (an electromagnet) is powered by an electric battery to turn the wheel of a toy car, but if we take the battery away and turn the wheel by hand we generate electricity through the rotation of the magnet.

Even if the Rous machine is absolutely impossible, this does not diminish the hardness of science in *The Blue World*, since by tradition, even the hardest of the hard sf is allowed one impossibility (especially if it is a linchpin for the story).

•

Back on the Blue World, there is a local mystery about copper. In their voyage of exile, Sklar's group first discovered a float of exiles from a much earlier generation, a group of people who had lost all traces of civilization and lived as preliterate tribes. Yet this group had possession of copper. Did they get all of it by killing kragen? If so, how did such non-technological people succeed against kragen? Sklar's people spy upon the mysterious savages and learn that the source of their copper is the husks of food sponges.

This has a satisfying feel to it. Not all the answers are discovered by one generation's golden season of experimentation and tinkering: some are accidental, and at least one is "stolen" from "primitives."

After more work, Sklar's group generates ten pounds of iron (from their own blood), fifty-five pounds of copper (from kragen blood and sponge husks), twenty-four flasks of acid of salt.

In addition to the copper blood, kragen corpses provide a wealth of previously untapped resources: their hides can be used to build fireproof boat hulls (16), and "splines" from their turrets are fashioned into another new device, the bow (15).

The ultimate device to kill King Kragen is a barge-mounted pair of large crossbows, armed with two iron harpoons, both trailing copper wire leading back to two hundred and ten voltaic cells.

Necessity being the Mother of Invention, the iconoclasts of the bone age world thereby discover metallurgy, glass, acid, and the generation of electricity. Having killed the parasitic god monster, they now have been released from feeding it and subsequently have a food surplus, freeing people from food production to pursue careers in hard science research or any of the new industries just created. The next big quest will undoubtedly be the hunt for and salvage of the starships that brought their ancestors to this planet.

## Soft SF: Onomastics and Sociolinguistics

In addition to the gritty hard science of *The Blue World,* we have the more usual Vancean treatment of soft science, this time in the form of speculative sociolinguistics. A familiar and fertile ground for Vance: his novel *The Languages of Pao* (1958) performs a vast experiment wherein a backwater planet with a homogeneous population is linguistically divided into specialist castes that transform their world into a stellar powerhouse at the cost of planetary unity ("The Power of Babble," you might say).

The reader of *The Blue World* quickly grasps the shameful origins of the colonists, of which they themselves are unaware, because the clan names are all criminal types: Smuggler, Felon, Blackguard, Hoodwink, etc. Twelve generations ago their ancestors were convicted criminals being transported to a prison world — the colonists know that the world they are on is not the target world "New Ossining," because, as one person puts it, "compared with our original destination this world is heaven" (35). It seems that the prisoners overpowered the crew and crashed the ships into the Blue World.

Okay, so *The Blue World* is also a cross of Botany Bay and *Mutiny on the Bounty.* And the reader is set up to anticipate a society-shaking revelation whenever somebody figures it all out (all bets being placed on the hero to do this).

Now watch closely. We've got all these criminals set loose on a tropical paradise where, in order to survive, they have to evolve a bone age civilization. Tasks have to be defined and assigned; people must work together for the good of the colony: ropes must be made, boats must be devised, fish must be caught, and shelter must be built, etc.

And this is where the Vancean magic takes place — because it turns out that each criminal designation gave linguistic hints and roles in the new world. The pinnacle being the caste of semaphorists, known as Hoodwinks (since the semaphore signals are sent by "winking" hoods over candle lights).

## TABLE OF CASTES

| Name | Crime | New Role | Rank |
|------|-------|----------|------|
| Advertisermen | unknown | Deep Divers | low |
| Anarchists | Anarchists | (extinct) | |
| Bezzlers | Drunkards | Water Engineers | high |
| Blackguards | Vagabonds | Arbor Builders | |
| Extorters | Blackmailers | Unknown but extant | |
| Felons | Major Crimes | Boat Builders | |
| Forgers | Forgers | They became Scriveners | |
| Goons | Fighters | (extinct) | |
| Hoodwinks | Con-Men | Semaphorists | high |
| Hooligans | Minor Crimes | Net makers | low |
| Incendiaries | Arsonists | Rope makers | high |

| Name | Crime | New Role |
|------|-------|----------|
| Jacklegs | Lawyers | Unknown but extant |
| Larceners | Thieves | Tower builders |
| Malpractors | Physicians | Tooth pullers |
| Nigglers | Coin shavers | Wood carvers |
| Perculators | Embezzlers | Dye works |

| Procurers | Pimps | Virtually extinct, stoics |
|-----------|-------|---------------------------|
| Scriveners | Loan sharks | Penmen |
| Smugglers | Smugglers | Varnish boilers |
| Swindlers | Cheats | Coracle fishermen |

It is a classic thought experiment, giving a segment of society a free reign and seeing the sort of civilization they create for themselves. *Lord of the Flies* (1954) comes to mind, but for "criminals in charge" we must turn to Kornbluth's *The Syndic* (1953), where organized crime governs the former U.S.A. Still, the primitivism of *Lord of the Flies* is closer to *The Blue World* than the vaguely "libertarian" feudalism of *The Syndic*.

In *The Blue World* each float is lead by an Arbiter (elected chief), with an Intercessor (priest) as second-in-command. These roles are open to any caste — even a low-caste Hooligan can become Intercessor (15), but in fact many Intercessors come from the high caste of Bezzlers (56). (Note that "Arbiter" can be read as "Judge," and "Intercessor," while perfect as "Priest," also has shades of "Lawyer," where judges and lawyers are elements from the colonists' collective criminal past.) The Arbiter has rank equal to craft masters and caste elders.

On the Blue World the criminal role becomes noncriminal through a punning transformation — this is obvious by the way that hoodwink becomes hood wink. That the Blackguards now make arbors that "guard" the food sponges in the "black" of water at night (against such small monsters as the kragen that raids Sklar's arbor) makes a vague sort of sense; that the Incendiaries have a monopoly on the preparation of fibers (where they formerly lit fuses) and the laying of ropes is clear cut; that coin clipping Nigglers became woodcarving artisans is fitting. Do I stretch too far in seeing that the "muck" of pre-boiled varnish is etymologically linked to the "mug" of "smuggler"? Did the Larceners become bamboo-frame tower builders because "steal" is close to the "steel" frames used in construction on the homeworld? (Or is "larceny" somehow more like "lashing"?) How did Hooligans come to make nets? ("Wool-igans"? "Haul-igans"?) And what sort of criminal is an "advertiserman," anyway (if not the vilified Madison Avenue man)?

The whole book is built upon clever puns: "Sklar Hast owned a small pad," we are told.

**Iron and Irony: or The Ecology of Wild Cars**

Through my soon-to-be-patented "school of over-reading," *The Blue World* was revealed to be part *Thumbelina* and part *King Kong* over a firm iconoclastic foundation of *The Gods of Mars,* yet an offhand statement by Don Simpson added a new angle. Originally I thought "kragen" was just a variant or slurring of "kraken," the famous sea monster; but Simpson recently informed me that he detects a vast amount of regional punning in Vance's work, the point here being that "Kragen" is a chain of auto parts suppliers. "So?" says I, only later making the connection that after killing kragens, the people use them for parts.

The kragen turret, with two eyes forward, two eyes back, mimics the lights of a car: "lenses of tough crystal behind which flickered milky films and a pale blue sheen" (47). Below this turret, the "black [horizontal] cylinder housing the maw [with attendant mandibles and palps] and the digestive process, below this the great flat sub-body — a rectangle" (47). And of course, the four propulsive vanes imitate the four wheels of a car.

Early on, an observer notes: "If we could cut it up, the parts might be of some use" (44). Kragen (auto) parts!

It seems so obvious that I began to wonder if I was the last one to learn a common observation. So I checked a couple of reviews (*F&SF, Analog*) as well as my Vance reference books, and found no hint.

The kragens really are like American cars of the 1950s. Perhaps they are modeled specifically after the Edsel, famous flop of 1957: its unique "horse collar" radiator grill translates directly into the maw of the kragen, with additional radiator chrome coming to life as the mandibles and palps which feed this monstrous mouth.

But if kragens are cars, then *The Blue World* is somehow an encrypted ecological parable: mixing eco-friendly auto dismantling and "kill your car" attitudes with eco-unfriendly whale killing practices.

It is ironic that the tropical islanders worship cars.

It is ironic that Sklar Hast and his followers are declared "criminal" when all humans on the Blue World are descended from criminals.

It is ironic that in killing kragens the bone-age people unconsciously imitate atomic-age automobile parts recyclers.

Is it ironic that in killing the Serpent of Eden, the people finally lift the curse of thirteen generations and free themselves from a prison they thought they had escaped? Vance novels are often about Justice (a big topic right there), and *The Blue World* is no exception. It does not seem to be an exaggeration to say that the prisoners inadvertently built their own cage and stayed within it until they had worked off the debt of their crimes.

If kragens are cars, then King Kragen must be Detroit, making it "Detroit versus Ecotopia;" or does "Detroit" here just stand for the Military Industrial Complex: another coddled octopus that grows large enough to become tyrannical? (This resonates with the fact that kragen parts make military hardware.)

With regard to the stunning revelation of their society's criminal origin, a society-shaking secret the reader is aware of from the first page — it never materializes. Meril, Sklar Hast's girlfriend, may have figured out the truth about the Firsts (172), but we don't hear what she tells Sklar so we can't be sure. Reader anticipations thwarted again! And this in contrast to the *Analog* review, which concludes: "Unfortunately, 'what happens next' is totally predictable from page to page: to this extent the story is written to formula, and it suffers in consequence" (166). (Of course every reader is entitled to an opinion, but still I'd question the opinion of any reviewer who made a point of wondering how the float-dwellers could make fire without having any rocks — I was never a boy scout, myself, yet even I know that there are fire-making techniques using sticks.)

**Summation and Aloha**

*The Blue World* is one of my favorite Vance novels, and I feel that it has been neglected because, even after some digging around, I have seen very little written about it, and nothing in any depth.

The science is intriguing; the society is simply amazing. There is also courtroom drama, espionage, daring raids, social revolution, and reactionary upheaval. Wonderful seafood, strong drink, good companionship.

****

**Bibliography**

Merril, Judith. "Review of *The Blue World* by Jack Vance." *Magazine of Fantasy & Science Fiction,* December 1966, 32–33.

Miller, P. Schuyler. "Review of *The Blue World* by Jack Vance." *Analog,* March 1968, 166.

Parmentier, Gregg (ed.). *The Vance Phile* No. 1–5 (fanzine). Parm Press, Iowa City, Iowa. 1993-1995.

Rawlins, Jack. *Demon Prince: the Dissonant Worlds of Jack Vance.* Borgo Press, San Bernardino, California. 1986.

Stephensen-Payne, Phil and Gordon Benson, Jr. *Jack Vance: A Fantasmic Imagination (Galactic Central Bibliographies Vol. 28).* Second Revised Edition. Galactic Central, Leeds, England. 1990.

Underwood, Tim and Chuck Miller (editors). *Jack Vance* (Writers of the 21st Century Series). Taplinger Publishing Company, New York. 1980.

Vance, Jack. *The Blue World.* Ballantine Books, New York. 1966.

# THE ADVENTURES OF JACK VANCE
# IN TRAVELING AND WRITING

Jack Vance has a way with worlds. Like a Zen illustrator using simple lines to portray a wondrous landscape, Vance uses a light touch to depict fictional cultures that are humorously, hauntingly, true and fitting. He conveys a deep understanding of human societies and their foibles, giving him the aura of being a jocular cultural anthropologist, a well-traveled man of the world.

The key seems to be that in Jack Vance a vivid imagination was aided and abetted by very real travel.

Toward the end of the autobiographical *This Is Me, Jack Vance,* the author writes, "much of my work was produced while [wife] Norma, [son] John, and I inhabited some agreeable location here and there about the world" (187–88). It seems as though this was a lifestyle he had dreamed of as a child in California while living in a ranch house where he could look up from the latest issue of *Weird Tales* to see Mount Diablo to the south: a romantic, dashing vision of traveling to exotic locations and writing exciting fiction, an adventure he was able to put into practice through five trips from around 1950 to 1974.

But first he went through two phases of more limited travel and writing, one at sea and one on land. Jack Vance was in the merchant marine for World War Two (1943-45), where he served on eight ships, visiting such places as Australia, the Solomon Islands, New Guinea, and Chile (*Me,* 72, 75). Shore leave provided the only time for visiting foreign lands, the majority of the time being spent on a ship at sea. During his shipboard time, Vance wrote what would later become three books (65): the six fantasy stories that make up *The Dying Earth* (1950), and the mystery novels *Take My Face* (a.k.a. *The Flesh Mask* 1957) and *Isle of Peril* (a.k.a. *Bird Island* 1957). Even though he had invested the time and effort, the works in question would not bear fruit for many years.

After the war he returned to Berkeley, where he met and married Norma (*née* Ingold) in 1946. While visiting his in-laws in Colton, Southern California, Vance tried an experiment of rapid production wherein he wrote the first two Magnus Ridolph stories in two days (87). Vance quickly abandoned the technique, but in contrast to the fate of his shipboard writing, the fate of this crop proved to be as momentous as the shot from a starting gun: the first three Magnus Ridolph stories were published in 1948, and Twentieth Century Fox bought the film rights for one of them ("Hard-Luck Diggings"). Vance went to work at Fox Studios for a time, but when that collapsed, the couple used the Hollywood money he had made to embark on their first trip abroad.

Jack and Norma travelled to England, Austria, and Italy. This was in "the late 1940s" (89) or it might have been the early 50s (David B. Williams writes in his online Biographical Sketch that it was in 1951). During a month or so in the Alps, Vance wrote "several novelettes and started *Vandals of the Void*" (92), the latter being a contracted novel. Then followed three weeks in Vienna, a visit to Venice, and a stay in Positano, where he finished *Vandals,* which would be published in 1953.

It is a challenge to guess at the titles of the novelettes written on this trip, since it is not entirely clear when the couple was in Europe and how quickly Vance's work was being published. Nevertheless, here is a list of his novelettes published from 1950 to 1953 (there were none in 1949):

1950: "To B or Not to C or to D" (a Magnus Ridolph case)
1951: "The New Prime" and "The Phlagian Siphon" (a.k.a. "The Uninhibited Robot")
1952: "Cholwell's Chickens" and "Sabotage on Sulpher Planet"
1953: "DP!," "Four Hundred Blackbirds," "The World Between," and "Sjambak"

"Four Hundred Blackbirds" and "The World Between" are very clearly analogs of the Cold War in Europe. "DP!" involves new displaced persons (called "DPs" in the World War Two era) appearing out of nowhere in Cold War Austria. The other novelettes have no clear connections to the places visited.

In 1953 the Vances formed a sort of writers' colony in Mexico for a month or two with Frank Herbert and his family (108); David B. Williams pegs this as beginning in September. Vance wrote "some short stories" and started the novel *Clarges,* which would be published as *To Live Forever* (1956). Both Vance and Williams suggest there were no sales, which caused the colony to collapse, but short stories published within a few years after this trip are:

1954: "First Star I See Tonight" (pub "The Absent Minded Professor") and "When the Five Moons Rise"
1955: "The Devil on Salvation Bluff" and "The Gift of Gab"
1956: "The Phantom Milkman" and "Where Hesperus Falls"

"The Devil on Salvation Bluff" is about the difficulties a colony of interstellar missionaries have in telling basic time on a world with multiple suns — it may draw upon the stereotype of the difference between precise time measurement in the States and the more laid-back sense of time in Mexico.

Upon returning to the USA, Jack and Norma started building their house in the Oakland hills, a process that would continue for decades.

The travel-bug bit again in 1957, sending the couple to Western Europe and Western Africa. Williams reports this trip as beginning in the summer, and according to *This Is Me,* they first went to Barcelona in Spain, and then to the Mediterranean island Ibiza, followed by two months on the Canary Islands (113). Traveling in Western Africa, Mr. and Mrs. Vance almost got to fabled Timbuktu, but had to turn back due to lack of funds. *This Is Me* gives no hints as to the fiction worked upon during this period, but the publishing history shows the following:

1957: "A Practical Man's Guide," "The House Lords," and *The Languages of Pao*
1958: "Coup de Grace" (a Magnus Ridolph case), "The Miracle Workers," "Parapsyche," "Ullward's Retreat," and *Slaves of the Klau* (a.k.a. *Gold and Iron*)
1959: "Dodkin's Job"

I do not detect much of a connection between the places and the fiction, in this case, except for the linkage of Western Africa with slavery in the U.S., and how slavery, both in the U.S. and among the stars, is part of *Slaves of the Klau,* one of Vance's most brutal books.

The fourth trip found the Vance family, now a trio with son John (born in 1961), in Tahiti during 1965. Among Vance's writings at this location is *The Last Castle* (116) published in 1966. For others, I can only guess:

1966: *The Eyes of the Overworld,* "The Secret," and *The Last Castle*

1967: *The Palace of Love,* "The Narrow Land," "The Man
 From Zodiac" (a.k.a. "Milton Hack from Zodiac"), and
 *The Pleasant Grove Murders*
1968: "Sulwen's Planet" and *City of the Chasch*

"The Secret" feels like it is set in a traditional island
culture in the South Pacific, and "The Narrow Land" maybe
has a trace of the tropics to it, but the other pieces seem far
removed. *The Blue World,* where humans live upon giant lily
pads on a water planet, was published in 1966 — perhaps
written by Vance in anticipation of visiting Tahiti.

In 1969 came a big trip, this time a grand tour of Europe
with a bit of South and Central America as well. The family
Vance visited the UK, Ireland, France, Spain, Portugal,
Dalmatia, Greece, Bulgaria, Romania, Hungary, Austria,
Germany, Panama, and Columbia (138–42). Jack Vance's
output here is mainly novels:

1969: *Emphyrio, The Dirdir, The Deadly Isles,* and *Servants of the
 Wankh*
1970: *The Pnume*
1971: *The Faceless Man* (a.k.a. *The Anome*)
1972: *The Brave Free Men*
1973: *Trullion: Alastor 2262, The Asutra, Bad Ronald,*
 "Morreion," and "Rumfuddle"

*Emphyrio,* where aloof alien overlords maintain peace in
war-scarred cities on planet Halma, might reflect echoes of
post-war Europe. *The Faceless Man* and sequel *The Brave Free
Men* involve, at some level, thoughts of federation, mixing
the dreamy potential of a United Europe with the prosaic
realities found in the United States; but *The Deadly Isles* is a
mystery set in the South Pacific (not a location on this
excursion).

The Vance family had their biggest trip five years later,
in 1974, when they went on a truly world-spanning tour.
Starting in Ireland, they visited France and Spain and spent

a month on the island Madeira (north of the Canary Islands); then on to South Africa, Rhodesia (149); followed by Karachi in Pakistan, three months on a houseboat on Nagin Lake in India, a month in Sri Lanka; then Singapore, Sumatra, Bali, and Borneo. Again there are no clues as to what was written during this long voyage away from the States, so I resort to listing what was published:

1974: *The Gray Prince* (a.k.a. *The Domains of Koryphon*), "The Seventeen Virgins," and "Assault on a City" (a.k.a. "The Insufferable Red-headed Daughter of Commander Tynnott, O.T.E.")

1975: *Showboat World* (a.k.a. *The Magnificent Showboats of the Lower Vissel River, Lune XXIII South, Big Planet*), *Marune: Alastor 933,* and "The Dogtown Tourist Agency"

1976: *Maske: Thaery*

*The Gray Prince* has the stamp of apartheid South Africa on it, with human colonists and displaced autochthons. I find *Marune* has a lot of Scotland about it, specifically castles in the highlands, but maybe I am just mistaking an Irish quality. Then again, "The Dogtown Tourist Agency" is set mainly on a planet bordering three interstellar empires, where the city is divided into three separate sectors along with a Cold War sort of feel, which makes it seem like an analog for Berlin in divided Germany — a country not on this particular itinerary. "Assault on a City" is set in what seems like a future San Francisco.

After this epic voyage, Jack Vance's trips were mainly to science fiction conventions where he was guest of honor (157). He mentions Canada, Australia, the Netherlands, Sweden, France, and Germany (158). Further research confirms he was guest of honor for at least three gatherings outside the United States: Vancouver SF Convention 7 in 1979, Hillcon in Rotterdam in 1981, and Tschaicon in Melbourne in 1982. These excursions were international, but certainly of shorter duration than those of the previous series. His travels were further curtailed when he was diagnosed with glaucoma in the mid-1980s.

Still, he had managed to take five extended trips abroad, and the experience of living in foreign lands undoubtedly had a strong influence upon the "cultural anthropology" aspect that is such a recognizable trait of Vancean fiction. The cosmopolitan worlds of Alphanor and Quantique; to the houseboat cultures of Sirene and Zeck; the bucolic villages of Moudervelt and Fluter; to the aristocratic diarists of Fader and Marune; the man-hunting artists of Terce — all of these, and more, inspired by the travel adventures of Jack Vance.

•

Post Script: Further notes discovered after the article's initial publishing:

• From the introduction to the collection *Dark Side of the Moon* (1986), Jack Vance writes that "DP!" was composed at the village Fulpmes in Austrian Tyrol where Vance was stung by a bee while sitting on the sunny balcony of the hotel. Vance reports that he and Norma revisited the village "last year" (1984). [My article shows this as a likely one — now it is known.]

• "The Phantom Milkman" derives from events at Kenwood, California, where the Vances and the Herberts were staying prior to the Mexico trip. Thus it was probably written in Mexico. [My article shows this as a likely Mexico written story, and now even more likely.]

• From the editor's introduction to the collection *Hard-Luck Diggings,* "DP!" was written at Fulpmes in 1951, as was *Vandals of the Void.*

\*\*\*\*

**Works Cited**

Stephensen-Payne, Phil and Gordon Benson, Jr. *Jack Vance: A Fantasmic Imagination: Galactic Central Volume 28 (Second Edition).*

Albuquerque, New Mexico: Galactic Central, 1990.

Vance, Jack. *This Is Me, Jack Vance! (Or, More Properly, This is "I").* Burton, Michigan: Subterranean Press, 2009.

Williams, David B. "Biographical Sketch." Vance Museum. <www.vancemuseum.com/vance_bio_1.htm>. Accessed 10 September 2013.

# TRACING TERMS IN JACK VANCE'S "SJAMBAK"

Through his science fiction Jack Vance presents alien worlds and establishes their cultural verisimilitude by using exotic terms that somehow seem real rather than made up. In most cases I don't know how he does it, but there are a few points where I get a hint of what he did.

Take the novelette "Sjambak" (1953). It describes an airless world named Cirgamesç, colonized by Javanese, Malay, and Arab settlers who live in domed-over valleys in the mountains. The story has these primary four alien terms:

*Sjambak* — a type of bandit/wizard who lives outside in the vacuum.
*Adak* — an obstacle to an irresistible emotion that leads to turbulence.
*Amok* — a person who, faced by an adak, resorts to killing.
*Napaû* — a philosophy where one finds meaning, life, and beauty in every aspect of the world.

These terms probably seem real because they actually *are* real, albeit altered in meaning.

*Sjambak* is a misspelling of "sjambok" [SHAM-bäk], an Afrikaans word for "whip," derived from Malay *cambuk.* The whip has no direct application to the Vance story, but the Malay connection rings out.

*Amok* is, of course, our "amok," from the Malay word *mengamuk* for a type of murderous psychological state. In *mengamuk,* first the person goes through a phase of inward-turning and indifference, then bursts out in a killing rampage against animals or people nearby, followed by a collapse into lethargy, from which he (or she) emerges with no memory of the event. Vance has recast this word from a mental state into a person. Vance is quite fascinated by the psychology of *amok,* and revisits it a number of times in his fiction: *awaile* among the Cath of Tschai (in the *Planet of Adventure* series) is identical in result but triggered by shame; *tamsour* on Ushant (in the novel *Night Lamp)* is exhibitionist suicide triggered by mid-life crisis.

*Adak,* however, is not a term from the psychology of amok. True amok seems to arise from a loss (loss of a companion, loss of economic or social prestige, etc.). Vance is casting his culture's berserk rage as a result of a blockage against impulse rather than a reaction to loss, and so he comes up with this word *adak* to describe it. *Adak* is another Malaysian word, meaning "unnecessary," but that seems incidental. To people of Vance's generation, "adak" would instantly bring to mind Adak Island. This Alaskan isle had a military base in World War Two, when it was next to two islands where the Japanese landed on American soil. This "Adak" was certainly a blockage against the Japanese impulse to conquer American territory.

Vance's *napaû,* which seems to be the opposite of the nihilistic *amok* state, has a similar forked root. "Napau" is Javanese for "why," but it is also the name of a crater trail among volcanoes in Hawaii. Craters might be important to Vance's vision because the settlements of planet Cirgamesç are all in mountain valleys that have been roofed over. (Adak Island also has a volcano.)

No doubt you are curious about the word "Cirgamesç" — aren't we all? This planetary name is mainly used in the story as a joke, where tourists try to puzzle out how to pronounce it: two "wrong" ways are "Sirgamesk" and "Hrrghameshgrrh." I can't find any trace of it outside of the story, so perhaps Vance made it up entirely.

So it seems to me that Vance took these Malay-derived words (amok, sjambok) and added them to some Malay words (*adak, napau*) that might also provide geographical associations he had for the world he was telling about. In three out of four cases he reassigned meaning completely, and even in the case of *amok* he changed it a bit.

There may be an additional layer of wordplay going on — for example, *sjambak* might be a cover for "sham buck," and truly the story deals with a fake cowboy of a most unusual sort — a figure who somehow rides a horse into orbit without a spacesuit. Perhaps this is a limb too far.

# PATTERNS TO THE FIVE DEMON PRINCES OF JACK VANCE

Jack Vance (1916–2013) brought many different angles to his fiction: he was a musician and an engineer, a cynical scoffer and a sensitive poet, a mystery crafter and an impish joker. So sometimes in Vancean fiction we find relatively straightforward patterns as in the case of the Lyonesse trilogy (which uses mythic places of Arthurian legend, such as Lyonesse, Ys, and Avalon), while other times a pattern flickers enigmatically on the border of order and chaos.

For example, take the eponymous villains of the Demon Princes series (1964–1981). There seems to be a pattern to these five galactic crime lords, but it is elusive. Over the course of five novels (*Star King, The Killing Machine, The Palace of Love, The Face,* and *The Book of Dreams*) we learn about each of the fellows in turn — they are all of a type (highly successful criminals), and while there is a certain amount of overlap in their characteristics, each is distinctive. I present them in the order of their novels:

• Malagate the Woe is different for being an alien Star King disguised as a human. His mode, therefore, is one of anonymity through camouflage. His goal is to obtain a new unsettled world where he can be his true self, and there become an Adam for a new race.

• Kokor Hekkus is a human transformed centuries before into a sort of vampire. He has access to a lost primitive planet where he plays many character roles, both high and low. His focus is on using Fear upon others, and to this end he has commissioned the terrifying "killing machine" that is both the name of his volume and the meaning of his name.

• Viole Falushe is a sex fiend who is impotent. His mode is flamboyant. He has a famous Palace of Love where he secretly tries again and again to capture the girl who, in real life, "got away."

• Lens Larque is a love-lorn trickster who wants to shape a world as a monument to lost love.

• Howard Alan Treesong is magic with insanity or insane with magic. Treesong has a multiplicity of "paladins" (actual spirits or imagined personalities) at his disposal. He wants to become the first galactic emperor through playing multiple character roles in public.

I don't want what follows to be seen as some literary chart like the Gilbert schema for James Joyce's *Ulysses,* where, for example, each chapter of that novel is linked to an organ of the human body. At this moment I'm not making a highbrow argument; I am not trying to elevate the artistry of Jack Vance; I'm only trying to get through the riddling of the trickster Jack Vance, which requires that one must be aware of the lowbrow as well.

Because they are called "demon" princes, one thinks immediately of the Seven Deadly Sins (Wrath, Greed, Sloth, Pride, Lust, Envy, and Gluttony) and the demons associated with them. Neither Sloth nor Gluttony seems to apply —

there is no "Jabba the Hutt" among Vance's demon princes
— which conveniently brings the number down to five, but
while "Lust" fits Falushe, and "Pride" fits Larque, there are
no other immediate matches. (Treesong's paladins number
seven, which might match up to the deadly sins, but still,
that's Treesong, not the demon princes as a group.)

There are touches of the Eurasian warlord to a couple of
the demon princes: Malagate's first name is "Attel," rather
close to Attila the Hun, who threatened the Roman Empire
in the fifth century; Falushe's "Palace of Love" has a clear
echo of the "stately pleasure dome" built by a later Mongol
emperor in Coleridge's famous poem "Kubla Khan." But
the demon princes do not appear to be based upon the
greatest Eurasian warlords (e.g., from Attila to Tamerlane).

It is fairly common to note that Vance's demon princes
are all frustrated artists of different mediums. Malagate's
quest shows him literally seeking Truth (his true self) and
Beauty (an Edenic world), and his hideously scarred
underling is ironically called "Beauty" Dasce. Hekkus has
played "theater" for 300 years on his lost medieval planet.
Falushe's medium is one of sensations epicurean, sybaritic,
and pornographic. Larque is a mining engineer; Treesong is
a writer. Unfortunately these four or five different arts do
not clump into a ready association of muses or what-have-
you.

The five characters have certain overlaps that divide
them into three groups: Disguised Self, Hurt by Love, and
Combination. While they all use disguise, Malagate's goal is
to find a place where he can put aside the mask and be his
true self; Hekkus is the opposite, as he revels in playing
multiple selves. Falushe and Larque were both hurt by love,
Falushe at the beginning of his career, and Larque near the
end of his. Combining these two types is Treesong, who has
a strange sense of Self, is playing multiple roles in public,
and was also hurt by love in his youth. But this by itself does
not suggest a further association.

Having exhausted the easy patterns, there is the

possibility that the cryptic structure itself is more Vancean, an idiosyncratic creation. Fueling this notion is the fact that the Demon Princes series involves the reuse of a few elements from other Vance works (where "reuse" here signals an item of personal importance rather than a simple artistic shortcut). For example, *The Palace of Love* (1967) reuses the cloning strategy of "Cholwell's Chickens" (1952); *The Book of Dreams* (1981) reuses (or "pre-uses") the fantasy power-trip notebook found in the mysteries *Bad Ronald* (1973) and *The House on Lily Street* (1979). More importantly, the premise of one hero's quest against five tyrants is in the novel *The Five Gold Bands* (1950), where the antagonists are mutant overlords who collectively hold a monopoly on star drives, thereby keeping Earth a backwater planet. The Earthman hero solves the treasure hunt by visiting each mutant homeworld in this order:

### Five Mutant Races

- Eagles — tall, thin, with feather-hair.
- Badau — possessing hump-heads and short legs.
- Loristanese — a race of butter-colored merchants, possibly telepathic.
- Shaul — having flesh cowls.
- Koton — with saucer-eyes, they are famed for cruelty.

The mutants are, like the demon princes, of a type and yet distinctive, but there is no immediate linkage between the mutants and the demon princes. The strange eyes of the Koton raises the possibility of connection to the five senses (vision, hearing, smell, taste, and touch), but it goes no further than that.

All of this is too much thinking. Let's strip it all down to basics and suppose that the demon princes are each the fingers of a hand. There is even a passage in the text that points in this direction, a text within the text, a quotation from "*The Demon Princes* by Caril Carphen" that says,

In our cursory summary we have seen how each Demon Prince is unique and highly individuated, each displaying his characteristic style.

This is all the more remarkable in that the basic variety of possible crime is limited and can be numbered on the fingers. (*Star King,* chapter 10)

The article then goes on to list *six* basic crimes, but no matter. This pattern of five fingers shows immediate promise, since the fingers have all sorts of folklore associations — most immediately the vulgar middle finger and the heart-linked ring finger.

### Fingers Five

- Thumb — Malagate. The most different.
- Forefinger — Hekkus.
- Middle Finger — Falushe. Lust.
- Ring Finger — Larque. Love.
- Little Finger — Treesong.

Malagate, as the only true alien, seems good as the "thumb" of the group for that reason, but there is also a curious detail in the text of *Star King* alluding to "thumb" when the avenging hero finds Malagate's underling, Beauty Dasce, has a hidden planet he calls "Thumbnail Gulch" (*Star King,* chapter 9). In this way the text links Malagate to Thumb. In folklore the thumb does not have an immediate meaning — in American culture there is "thumbs up/down" for good/bad, a pointer for "me" (thumb to chest), and the hitch-hiker's gesture ... come to think of it, Malagate does hitch a ride to the Edenic planet in the avenger's starship.

Falushe as "middle finger" is perfect, while Larque as "ring finger" emphasizes the love rather than the pride, but this seems fitting, as Larque is the most sympathetic of all the demon princes.

Hekkus as the forefinger is plausible (a "trigger finger"

for the "killing machine"), but with Treesong as the little finger, things get very interesting.

It is time to examine Treesong's seven imaginary paladins. In his teenage notebook "The Book of Dreams," he lists them in a specific order, with "Immir," the one who represents Treesong himself, in the middle (*The Book of Dreams,* chapter 1). Each paladin is associated with a color, except for Immir ("the unpredictable").

### Colors Seven

- Eia (white)
- Rhune (blue)
- Rais (black)
- Immir (Treesong)
- Loris (red)
- Mewness (green)
- Spangleway (yellow)

These are basic colors, but they do not match the rainbow's spectrum (red, orange, yellow, green, blue, indigo, violet). Instead they are colors associated with the days of the week in a fairly widespread occult system (c.f. Buckland's *Complete Book of Witchcraft,* 2002, "Table 3: Days of the Week"), where Sunday is yellow (for the Sun), Monday is white (for the Moon), Tuesday is red (for Mars), and so on.

### Days and Colors

- Sunday: Yellow
- Monday: White
- Tuesday: Red
- Wednesday: Purple
- Thursday: Blue
- Friday: Green
- Saturday: Black

Treesong's list is not in "weekday" order, instead being arranged with abstraction colors (white, blue, black) to one side of him and life colors (red, green, yellow) to the other side. Within this "days of the week" scheme, the missing color/day for "Immir" is purple/Wednesday, which is tied to planet Mercury. By a spooky twist, in palmistry the little finger is also associated with Mercury.

Mercury seems to be a superb link to Treesong. His

character is clearly "mercurial" in the prosaic sense of his being subject to sudden or unpredictable changes of mood or mind. The element mercury is associated with madness, commonly enough that hat makers who were frequently exposed to mercury in the felting process were prone to "Mad Hatter disease." The god Mercury was also a psychopomp, a messenger to and from the spirit world, and this captures Treesong's weird conversations with the paladins as being true (rather than mere madness). In this way, mercury embodies Treesong's flighty, manic behavior as well as both sides of the madness/magic question.

This is not the only time Vance has played with the seven day pattern: in one of his Gaean Reach novels (*Araminta Station,* chapter 1) he gives the "Metallic Schedule" for the Gaean Week, basically showing how each day is named after a metal. He neglects to show how this seemingly arbitrary (and "culturally neutral") scheme closely matches up to our own week (using the "Chaldean System," a fairly widespread occult system of the Western World):

**Metallic Schedule: the Gaean Week**

| Name | Metal | Western Day |
|---|---|---|
| Ort | Iron | Tuesday |
| Tzein | Zinc | n/a |
| Ing | Lead | Saturday |
| Glimmet | Tin | Thursday |
| Verd | Copper | Friday |
| Milden | Silver | Monday |
| Smollen | Gold | Sunday |

Again we see that the order has been scrambled and notice the special treatment meted out to Wednesday, where zinc has been substituted for quicksilver. This directly matches the list of Treesong's paladins (where the color for Wednesday is obscured), and thus appears to be a true

Vancean pattern.

So it seems the five demon princes each represent a different finger and a different mental state: Malagate is called "the Woe," which initially seems to be about the sadness he causes his victims, but in the end is his own; Hekkus is about Fear; Falushe focuses on Lust; Larque has his monumental Pride; and Treesong is a study of Insanity.

### Finger Demon Focus & Art

| Digit | Demon Prince | State | Notes |
|---|---|---|---|
| Thumb | Attel Malagate | Woe | Pure Art |
| Forefinger | Kokor Hekkus | Fear | Theater |
| Middle Finger | Viole Falushe | Lust | Saturnalia |
| Ring Finger | Lens Larque | Pride | Love |
| Little Finger | Treesong | Insanity | Mercury |

All this brings us to the phrase "five against one," a slang term for male masturbation, famously used by Hemingway in *A Farewell to Arms* (1929). I do not wish to cause embarrassment by painstakingly listing multiple instances where Vance alludes to the solitary vice, but I should point to at least a couple of cases. The first is rather obscure, involving the woman-hating priests of Durdane and their drug-fueled rites (tip of the hat to David Langford's "Cloud Chamber 88" for this "jackpot"). The second is somewhat notorious, being the title of a Tschai novel, which proved to be of such lingering controversy among certain Vance fans that it recently was, rather shamefully, retitled as *The Wannek.*

No doubt this last bit seems like an outrageous stretch, even compared to the points before. In closing, I draw attention to the last paragraph of the Demon Princes series, a moment in which the avenger responds to the girl's concern about his health: "Quite well. Deflated, perhaps. I have been deserted by my enemies. Treesong is dead. The affair is over. I am done."

# "THE NEW PRIME" AS HERALD OF
# FUTURE JACK VANCE

Sometimes an artist produces an early piece that stands out from its neighbors as a prodigy, a bold example of what the artist will later become famous for. I will make the case for one such, Jack Vance's novelette "The New Prime" (1951), first published as "Brain of the Galaxy" in the magazine *Worlds Beyond*.

In the course of doing research for my compact reference aid *Handbook of Vance Space* (2014), I immersed myself in Vance's early work. His first publications were such space adventures as "The World Thinker" (1945), "Planet of the Black Dust" (1946), and "Phalid's Fate" (1946), all fairly rough-cut and generic. Stories and novels quickly followed, but "The New Prime" stands out to me as exemplifying Vance's work beginning ten years later with "The Moon Moth" (1961).

I can see why the editors at *Worlds Beyond* renamed "The New Prime" as "Brain of the Galaxy," since, spoiler alert, the whole story is about a galaxy-wide competition among candidates vying to become the next almost god-like ruler of the Milky Way, said role being the "new Prime" of the original title.

The story begins in twentieth-century Boston where our young hero, Arthur, finds himself in the nightmare situation of being naked at a public event. Then the story shifts to a more Beowulfian tale starring Bearwald, who is leading a platoon fighting against hive-building monsters. Then it shifts again to a blend of Barsoom and Arabian Nights where hero Ceistan drives his air-sled into the dead city, Therlatch. Another shift brings us Dobnor, participant in a technological magic contest wherein six adepts cast illusions at each other in an arena, building dreams. A fifth shift gives us Ergan, prisoner of war in a vaguely Renaissance level technology setting, who is tortured until his stubborn resistance becomes heroic.

The sixth turning pops us out into the frame tale, where Galactic Prime is the first to finish the test of running the gauntlet of these five wildly different scenarios. He is confident, as he should be since he designed the test. He has scored highest, but the judges refuse to grant him "a second span of authority" over the galaxy.

He reveals that the Earth phase tested social intuition and flexibility; the Beowulf part measured leadership; the Arabesque adventure assayed devotion to duty; the *battle royale* of techno-wizards investigated imagination; the prisoner's response to torture highlighted resolution.

So a quick list is in order.

1. Naked nightmare: Wodehouse mode.
2. Beowulf mode: leadership edging into bloodlust.
3. Barsoomian Arabesque mode.
4. Battle of Techno-Wizards: hymn to the craftsman.
5. Response to torture: heroic insanity.

I should tell about Vance's use of these modes across his work.

Vance uses the Wodehouse mode of light social comedy more often than one might suppose. The novel *Space Opera*

(1965) captures it well: an eccentric aunt, an awkward nephew as hero, and a series of social comedies. In the same vein are *Big Planet* (1957), *Showboat World* (1975), *Ports of Call* (1998), and *Lurulu* (2004).

The Beowulf mode where leadership edges into bloodlust is used in *Slaves of the Klau* (1958), probably Vance's most brutal work. Without the bloodlust factor we see straight up fantasy combat through technological means in *The Dragon Masters* (1962), *The Last Castle* (1966), and *The Asutra* (1974) of the Durdane trilogy.

The Barsoomian mode is close to the science fantasy of *The Dying Earth* (1950) but still on the sf side. Vance's four-volume *Planet of Adventure* quartet is generally acknowledged to be his homage to Barsoom. But in "The New Prime" he uses this for an Arabesque ghost story in the ruins: the dead city is in the desert; its notable buildings include a Mosque and a "Sumptuar," the later of which initially seems to be a temple of holy maidens, but by stages it comes to seem more like a civic brothel of temple prostitutes. This perfectly matches the Arabesque motif of tired travelers seduced by damsels who are disguised monsters. Note the lewdness that creeps into this third stage of the story, the middle of five. (The term "Sumptuar" seems to be a Vance coinage, somewhat like "sumptuous" but actually closer to "sumptuary," as in the sumptuary laws that regulate permitted consumption. Thus, "a place of lavish yet regulated consumption.")

Vance uses the Battle of Techno-Wizards many times, most notably in the Jinxmen of "The Miracle-Workers" (1958), as well as the psionic overlords in *Slaves of the Klau* and "Telek" (1952). But in "The New Prime" Vance uses the occasion to impart a hymn to the craftsman: for his final creation hero Dobnor builds a dream of a pebble carved into a woman's beautiful face, then magnified into a planet orbiting a beloved star. While this vignette finds echo in *The Face* (1979), Vance often touches on the craftsman and the art expression of love, for instance through the hero's father in *Emphyrio* (1969).

Heroic insanity features in many of Vance's works: the sf horror tale "When the Five Moons Rise" (1954), and the more "experimental" works "Noise" (1952) involving a lone survivor, and "The Men Return" (1957), revolving around an extreme reality shift.

My main point in highlighting this story is that it is a tour de force showing what Vance was capable of at an early point in his career and how he followed through in later years with at least the twenty works I have mentioned. "The New Prime" is like an artist's palette that way, having these different modes instead of paint blobs, allowing Vance to dazzle the reader with high variety in relatively short space. The ending has an unspecified number of twists that I will not give away, as much as I would like to do so.

But having come this close to the text, it appears that in addition to being the germ of Jack Vance, practically the quintessence, the novelette also contains the Vancean Pattern of Five, most fully expressed in the Demon Princes series. In another essay I surmised that Vance had a "fingers of the hand" thing going on in each of the Demon Princes, from thumb to little finger. The same pattern seems obvious here, from the insanity of the little finger, the love and craft of the ring finger, the lewd danger of the middle finger, the violence of the index finger.

### Vancean Pattern of Five

Thumb: *Star King:* Control
Index: *The Killing Machine:* Combat
Middle: *The Palace of Love:* Lust
Ring: *The Face:* Love and Crafting
Little: *The Book of Dreams:* Insanity

As such, "The New Prime" is a direct ancestor to the Demon Prince series, having far more bearing upon it than *The Five Gold Bands* (1953). Which further emphasizes the import of this one early piece to the entire body of Vance's work.

# REVIEW OF *AN ENCYCLOPEDIA OF JACK VANCE*

Michael Andre-Driussi, independent scholar (B.A. in English from U.C. Berkeley) with a specialization in the fictions of Gene Wolfe (*Lexicon Urthus* [1994]), Jack Vance (*Vance Space* [1997]), and John Crowley (co-editor of *Snake's-hands* [2003]). His fiction has appeared in *Interzone* and *Tomorrow SF;* his essays on sf have appeared in *Extrapolation, Foundation,* and *The New York Review of Science Fiction.*

•

Mead, David G. *An Encyclopedia of Jack Vance, 20th-Century Science Fiction Writer. Volume I: A-J.* Lewiston, New York: The Edwin Mellen Press, 2002. 460 pp. Hard cover (no dustjacket). ISBN 0-7734-7313-0. $129.95

*Volume II: K-N* . . . 164 pp. ISBN 0-7734-7222-3. $99.95

*Volume III: Numericals through -Z* . . . 381 pp. ISBN 0-7734-7224-X. $119.95

•

*An Encyclopedia of Jack Vance* "attempts to list and define all the people, places, and things invented by Jack Vance for his fiction in English. It contains somewhat more than 15,600 terms" (iii). This is a prodigious undertaking, to say the least: Jack Vance's career spans 58 years, so the three-volume *Encyclopedia* draws from 145 published source texts: everything from the novella "Abercrombie Station" to the novel *Wyst: Alastor 1716,* as well as the outline for *The Genesee Slough Murders,* a mystery novel that never got beyond the outline stage. (The editions cited are mainly the easiest-to-find ones, paperbacks from DAW and Ace, for example.) The only omission is the three novels written by Vance as Ellery Queen. The Vance Integral Edition also omits these, but only because Jack Vance does not hold copyrights. The *Encyclopedia* would be more useful with them included, particularly for comparison with Vance's other mysteries.

Author David Mead (Ph.D. in English from the University of Florida, 1975), a professor of English at Texas A&M University-Corpus Christi, is to be commended for his exhaustive research. Consider the following entry:

> **Soum.** 1) the "thick, tough, dun lichen which carpets most of the Palga" on Koryphon. **GP**, 90. 2) The word for the essential stuff of fairies. It is dissipated as fairies or halflings consume too much earthly or human food. **LM**, 173. 3) A geologically old world orbiting Vergaz in Mircea's Wisp. The Mummers of Cadwal perform here often. It is said later to orbit Mazda (**THR** 84), **ARS**, 46.

This entry on "Soum" establishes that the word has been used three times in very different contexts: two unrelated science fiction novels (*The Gray Prince* and *Araminta Station* [of *The Cadwal Chronicles*]) and a fantasy novel (*Lyonesse III: Madouc)*; that the word has a different meaning in each context (a lichen, an essence, the name of a planet); and finally there is a note about a textual inconsistency about the word in *The Cadwal Chronicles* (in *Throy*). This rich entry and many others like it allow us to peer over Vance's shoulder as he works his writing magic.

For another example of Vance reusing a term, consider the following entries:

**Simic.** A Baron of Scharrode; one of the eiodarks. **MA**, 149.
**Simic, Andrei.** 1) A man of Shant ... **ANO**, 158. 2) A Gaean
    philosopher ... **WY**, 221.
**Simic, SS Andrei.** A spaceship.... **HI**, 139.

In this case, "Simic" is the name of a noble in *Marune,* a man in *The Anome,* a philosopher in *Wyst,* and the name of a spaceship in *The Houses of Iszm.* One's curiosity becomes aroused: who is the real-life Andrei Simic?

Another entry showing unexpected correspondences is: "**Quantique.** 1) A cosmopolitan center of the Oikumene ... 2) A region of the Dying Earth." This exhibits in Vance's writing a crossover between science fiction (*Star King,* published in 1964) and fantasy (*Cugal's Saga,* published in 1983, thirty-three years after the publication of *The Dying Earth).*

The depth of the entries does not always correspond to their importance in Vance's oeuvre: "Olliphane," a very minor location in the Demon Princes series, receives 8 lines of text whereas the entry for "Pao," the main world of the novel *The Languages of Pao,* has only three lines. Such idiosyncrasies are natural to reference works of this type, however.

One puzzling section, at least to me, is the three page Numerical section of Volume 3. All phrases beginning with numerals are gathered here: stars ("1012 Aurigae"), streets, street addresses, telephone numbers, dates ("2 Ferario Gaean"), cabin numbers, and the like. I would have preferred to find these under the first word after the numerals, if there is one. Perhaps the numerals are useful to other researchers, however.

The *Encyclopedia* originated in the form of a computer database. In his "Commendatory Preface," Walter E. Meyers writes:

> Many of those readers [of Jack Vance] will be especially grateful that Mead decided to build his Encyclopedia from a computerized database, allowing easy updates and revisions. His decision makes the work doubly useful: the reader who wants a definition of "zipangote" or "monoline" will find satisfaction in the printed text; the one who wants a more general search — on "language," say, or "musical instrument" or "mask" — will find the electronic form indispensable.

The printed text therefore appears to be a pale shadow of the database version. Mead himself promotes the database as well: "In its electronic form, the data printed here can be searched and cross-referenced in a variety of ways, so that patterns hitherto available only to the most assiduous reader can be extracted quickly and comprehensively" (iii). Unfortunately, Mead tells me, he has not found a publisher for the CD-ROM version.

The database origin explains the position of the numericals, as well as weak cross-referencing in general. Cross-referencing is not totally absent: the entry for Phi Ophiuchi gives "A star with a single planet, Sarkovy"; the one for "Alastrid Goddesses" ends with "See: Cassadense, Giampara, Core of the Four Bosoms, Thaia"; and the entry under Oikumene includes "See: Commonwealth, System, Home Worlds, Gaean Reach." But some entries fall short: "Alphanor" lists "seven continents: Phrygia, Umbria, Lusitania, Sythia, Etruria, Lydia, and Lycia," but fails to mention "Trans-Iskanas," the southern continent, which has its own entry later in the text. Other cases more clearly show a lack of cross-referencing: "Half-aud" (an excellent test-word for any Vance reference work) is properly listed as a day-mode of the Rhunes, which is good, but there is no cross-reference to a list of all the modes (Aud, Isp, Chill Isp, Umber, Lorn Umber, Rowan, Red Rowan, Green Rowan, Mirk, etc.); the entry for the star "Komred" makes no mention of its planet "Verlaren"; the entry for the star "Miel" does not reference its planet "Sogdian."

In a reference book of this category there are bound to be typos, even more so in a multivolume work. I found two instances of incorrect citation codes: the entry under "Achernar" gives four different uses of the term, with the third case being "A star near Thamber **DIR**, 112" and the fourth case regarding an episode from "the scroll from the 9th Dimension **PL**, 202." But Thamber was not a part of DIR (*The Dirdir*), it was in KM (*The Killing Machine*); and the scroll episode in question was not in PL (*Palace of Love*), but in FA (*The Face*).

Also a simple typo, for "Hyaspis" we have "Fifth planet of Fritz's Star (Ceti 1920)" where it should be "Ceti 1620."

I found a few omissions: there is no entry for "Sagitta 203" (*Palace of Love,* ch. 3), but there is one for its other name, "Murchison's Star"; there is no entry for "Mizar VI" (mentioned in *Star King,* ch. 7); nor is there one for "Nova Bactria" (in *The Book of Dreams,* ch. 4).

But this is nit-picking: the number of mistakes I have listed (six, to include omissions) represent 4% of the 150 entries I studied closely, suggesting that the entire text is 96% accurate — a remarkable achievement.

In the end, the *Encyclopedia* succeeds at its goal: if a researcher knows the word, he or she can find it and learn more about it, exploring Vance's craft at the word level. There is no other book like this for studying Jack Vance. The nearest contender is Dan Temianka's *The Jack Vance Lexicon,* a slim volume of 1700 entries that focuses on words coined by Vance. The *Encyclopedia* is nine times the size, and while Mead admits his work "does exclude a few items (mostly nonsense words not susceptible to definition) which are included in *The Jack Vance Lexicon*" (iii), in comparison of the two works, the *Lexicon* gives only one reference for "Soum" (as opposed to the *Encyclopedia*'s three), and has no entry for either "Simic" or "Quantique."

This work is best suited for a college library as well as those among the legions of Jack Vance fans who can afford the price.

# ABOUT THE AUTHOR

Michael Andre-Driussi has written a number of science fiction reference books, from *Lexicon Urthus* (1994) to *Handbook of Vance Space* (2014). At about the midpoint of that range he co-edited with Alice K. Turner a sturdy *Snake's-hands: the Fiction of John Crowley* (2001). His fiction, published in venues from *Aberrations* to *Wicked Words Quarterly*, has been collected in *Fallout Stories* (2016), *Doomsday and Other Tours* (2016), and *The Jizmatic Trilogy* (2017). He has visited England, Belgium, the Netherlands, Germany, Austria, Italy, France, Monaco, Spain, Canada, Mexico, Hong Kong, Macao, Singapore, Japan, Switzerland, and the Virgin Islands.

www.ingramcontent.com/pod-product-compliance
Lightning Source LLC
Chambersburg PA
CBHW021143020426
42331CB00005B/877